Follow the
Story

Follow the Story

THE FOUNDATION
OF EVERY
GREAT ATTRACTION

WRITTEN BY SCOTT SWENSON
EDITED BY PHILIP HERNANDEZ

Copyright © 2019 by Philip L. Hernandez

Cover Illustration Copyright © 2019 by Doug Schaefer

First paperback edition July 2019

Foreward by Ted Dougherty
Cover Illustration by Doug Schaefer
Book & Cover design by iPublicidades.com

ISBN 978-1-7332733-0-5 (paperback)
ISBN 978-1-7332733-1-2 (ebook)

Published by Philip Hernandez
www.philiplhernandez.com

PRAISE FOR
Follow the Story

"I've been a fan of Scott's work since the early Howl-O-Scream days. This book is a fantastic glimpse into his process of creating memorable haunts. Every haunt creator will find something useful to take away from reading this.

A perfect blend of creative and logistical guidance, this book gives every haunt creator plenty of helpful takeaways."

- **RICKY BRIGANTE**, Pseudonym Productions

Contents

Foreward

It was just one click away...

Growing up here in Southern California, I've been fortunate to witness the rise in popularity of Halloween festivities at theme parks in my region. Visiting *Knott's Scary Farm* religiously every year is now a way of life for me. With the addition of *Universal Studios Hollywood Halloween Horror Nights, Queen Mary's Dark Harbor, Mickey's Halloween Party at Disneyland* and *Six Flags Fright Fest at Magic Mountain,* I've learned how our local companies approach Halloween with their diverse flavors and character.

While working my haunting formative years at *Knott's Scary Farm* as one of the 'sliding' monster characters, I also worked as an associate producer for a video-based media company that presented on-camera educational featurettes of Halloween events across the nation. Through this company, *Haunted Media Magazine*, I became more exposed to the array of haunted attractions the country has to offer. Between my early years at *Knott's* and my time documenting haunts as a producer, I felt I was gaining a nice handle on the steady growth of the haunting industry.

By the close of the 2000's, I began transitioning from being a character/actor to my current and professional role in the themed entertainment/Halloween industries as a writer, producer and director. I became more in tune with growing Halloween events around the world. It was around that time I started hearing murmurs of how good *Busch Garden's Howl-O-Scream* in Tampa, Florida was becoming. *Busch Gardens?* I knew very little about the park other than our local *Busch Gardens* in Van Nuys, Ca. closed years ago. However, my knowledge of their Halloween event was about to change.

A trusted industry colleague attended Tampa's *Howl-O-Scream* in 2010. Upon his return, he provided an in-depth, spoiler-free analysis of a new haunted house that debuted at *Howl* that year named *"Alone."* Apparently, guests had to go through this maze *alone*, which at that time, was unheard-of for a major Halloween theme park. I had so many questions about how this ambitious attraction operated…

My colleague explained: *Alone* was an upcharge (*What?! Nobody is going to pay even more money on top of park admission to go through a single maze! That'll never work!*); it was time-ticketed (*Holy cow! What an operational mess that must be!*); not only must you sign a waiver, there was a safe word if the experience becomes too intense (*What..? How dog gone scary is this thing?*); if you brave the entire maze alone, you get an exclusive t-shirt to show off the fact you made it out alive (*Whoa…wait a minute…that's interesting. They're actually challenging the guests*). My imagination was whirling with the possibilities of the terror hiding inside this experience.

I then asked myself a very serious question, *"Would I ever have the guts to go through a maze like this?"* I honestly didn't know. No safety net to fall back on. This attraction appeared to go against all the theme park rules I'd grown up with.

My brave, more reasonable side asked, *"How scary could this really be? What true level of fright can this possibly reach? They can't hurt me…right?"* This was before the majority of immersive horror experiences began to have a large impact on the Southern California market. I just never heard of such a thing – an upcharge theme park haunted house where you must go alone, a signed waiver and appointment is mandatory, a safe word is implemented and if, somehow someway, you don't chicken out, you get a t-shirt to brag that you survived.

Gosh darn it, I needed to do this!

I was so curious about this attraction that was *daring* me to go through it, I persuaded my dear wife and a couple close industry friends into taking a vacation the following October (2011) to bright and sunny Florida. We were on a mission…

Leading-up to that October, I excitedly waited for *Howl-O-Scream* tickets to go on sale and finally, the wait was over. I recall combing the *Busch Gardens* website to find the *Alone* reservation times and once my date/time was confirmed, credit card information entered and just about to click 'CONFIRM ORDER,' I paused...

I thought, *'Wait a minute. What in the world am I doing? Am I really going to travel across the country just so I can go through this haunted house? This is absurd!'* I was somehow being drawn to this attraction.

But more importantly, somewhere way deep down inside me, a smaller quieter voice whispered, *'Can you really do this? Do you have the guts to go through this maze?'* I was actually nervous. Sitting in our first little apartment in a suburb outside of Los Angeles on a hot summer day and over 2,500 miles away from a theme park in Florida I'd never been to, I was actually nervous and because of that tension, so help me, I was hesitant to do this.

It was just one click away....

My finger hovered over my computer mouse for a long moment as I pondered the mystique of this attraction but before I could change my mind, I clicked and purchased the tickets.

And *Alone* turned out to be one of the most fun theme park haunted houses I'd ever been through. Not to mention, *Howl-O-Scream* blew me away with its overall production, quality, professionalism and entertainment – they even had sliders like the ones we have at *Knott's Scary Farm*, which I had not yet personally witnessed at another park outside of California. It was a delightful trip I'll never forget.

The following year (2012), *Knott's Scary Farm* debuted *Trapped*, their first upcharge, time-ticketed maze to rave reviews. Not too long after that, other events began to join the fun for more immersive, personalized, up-charged and interactive experiences. The Halloween theme park industry started a new chapter. It turned out that *Alone* was a game-changer.

∽≫⊗∾

As I began more creative and design work in the Halloween and theme park industries, I eventually came across the name *Scott Swenson*. I ultimately learned the creation of *Alone* at *Howl-O-Scream* fell under Scott's umbrella. After Scott's work as Director of Creative Services at *Busch Gardens,* he went on to form *Scott Swenson Creative Development, LLC.* Over the past few years, I've been fortunate to become friends with Scott and I'm now able to hear his haunt stories and anecdotes, all of which have been very inspiring. So, when I was asked to write an introduction to this book, I accepted immediately.

The valuable information you hold in your hands has the capability to both spark creativity and educate most any haunter – from yard haunts, home haunts all the way up to large scale Halloween theme parks. The importance of *story* for any themed entertainment attraction cannot be overstated. In my profession, these details are the basis for every project I've worked on.

If you're looking at ways to create a richer experience for your guests, you've come to the right place. The information found in these pages includes tools that can help immerse your guests deeper into an adventure that will stick with them for years to come. With his thorough analysis, Scott shares his expertise in a thoughtful method that can be immediately applied to your work. I know it not only works as a refresher in my creative process, I certainly learned several tips along the way.

Admittedly, if Scott showed me anything, he demonstrates fear has no boundaries and if done right, can be triggered with something as simple as being…

…Just one click away.

Beast Wishes,

TED DOUGHERTY

Ted Dougherty is a writer, producer & director having worked with Knott's Scary Farm, Universal Studios Hollywood Halloween Horror Nights, Queen Mary's Dark Harbor, Cedar Fair, Plague Productions and Hollow Studios. Prior to authoring the award-winning book 'Knott's Halloween Haunt: A Picture History," Ted terrified thousands of guests at Knott's Berry Farm's famous Ghost Town Scare Zone.

Introduction

In the beginning...

As the sun disappears behind the jagged tree line, there's a spark...followed by another...and another. Delicate wisps of smoke twist from the pile of dried grass. Amber flames emerge—growing in size and strength. A band of primates has discovered fire! Fire provides warmth, light, and a place to cook food.

Fire also provides a place to gather and share knowledge. It's a place to tell stories.

Humans continue to gather around fires, tables, televisions, and computers to hear stories. Stories give our brains a structure for processing information. Once a person recognizes a story narrative, their brain shifts into learning mode. Focus and retention increase in the listener. They're more likely to develop emotional connections to the content. We, as a species, are hardwired to gather and process information through stories.

You may think, "This is interesting, but what does it have to do with attractions?" The answer is simple... EVERYTHING!

An attraction is most effective when it follows a path, when it takes guests on a journey. The story determines an attraction's physical layout, character development, and technical design. It also points the way for clever marketing, merchandising, and branding.

This book gives you the tools to develop a story and to use that story as a blueprint for your attraction's development.

CHAPTER 1

Understanding the Anatomy of Terror

CRAFTING THE STORY

Before we brainstorm about cannibalistic hillbillies or chainsaw-wielding clowns, let's define structure. It's simple. There's a beginning, a middle, and an end. Now, before you say to yourself, "Duh…I already know that," and skip to the next chapter, stay with me here. You'll come away with a better understanding of each component.

THE BEGINNING

The beginning of a story provides background. It establishes the reality. It "sets the scene." Sometimes, the beginning needs to be complex with much exposition and backstory. In other cases, it can be as simple as, "You're lost in the woods…" Either way, define the beginning.

Some attractions share the beginning via marketing before guests arrive. Others use the queue experience and have characters or video segments. Still others wait until the first scene or room to give context clues. The best haunted attractions do all three—and the weakest do none.

The beginning also acts as a transition from the real world into your haunt's world. It gives guests time to understand the new reality and what role they play in it. As the guests' first impression of the attraction, it needs to draw them in without giving away every secret. It needs to be basic enough to help guests understand what's about to happen yet strong enough to propel the story.

Let's use an example. Your story: A successful surgeon fails to save his beloved wife on the operating table. Guilt drives him homicidal. The beginning can include suggestions of the original practice and of his marriage. Your website displays well-worn love letters and date-night photos marred by bloody fingerprints. Your queue may be in the abandoned waiting room of his once-thriving office. The broken lights flicker as the off-pitch waiting music skips. Blood from scalpel slashes paints the wall. Surgical gauze binds the receptionist in the corner. Helpless, she's seen the surgeon do terrible things to his unsuspecting patients. She mutters, "He keeps cutting…he just keeps cutting…" as guests pass. These audiovisual clues define the backstory but reveal none of the terror ahead.

THE MIDDLE

The middle of your story is the real "meat and potatoes" of the attraction. It's a series of events that should grow in intensity until the climax. Each middle-story event pushes the guests to the next. Random scares aren't effective alone. Aligning story events has a cumulative effect—the fear grows in both intensity and believability.

There are two types of middle events: key moments and connecting scenes.

Key moments are the action-building events while connecting scenes are quiet moments. Connecting scenes create a sense of anticipation, give guests time to process the terror, and provide contrast for the next key moment. There's a lot going on in the middle section of your story. Let's review each element and how they fit together.

CONNECTING SCENES

Big scares lose impact without corresponding connecting scenes. This doesn't mean that nothing is happening in these scenes. They must be immersive enough to maintain the forward momentum of the story.

Example: Guests mentally leave the story when the connecting scenes are black, plywood hallways. The lack of atmosphere breaks your spell. It allows the guest's mind to wander out of the story. If doors line the same hallway (they need not be practical) and guests hear crying from behind the door at the end of the hallway, this sustains the story. Guests begin to ask questions about the story. Who's crying? Will one of these doors pop open? If one pops open, what will be behind it? By giving guests enough story content to spark their imaginations, you keep them immersed in your world. Some fans feel the anticipation is almost as much fun as the scare itself. It's a balance. The anticipation loses its appeal if there aren't any scary pay-offs.

Key Moments

Key moments must grow in intensity. Key Moments may start quiet and get louder each time. They may also start small and get bigger or more violent or more disgusting than the last. Use a combination of tactics to build the intensity of these scenes.

The story births key moments. Back to the tale of our insane surgeon... A chainsaw-wielding actor in a rabbit costume will startle guests but is outside the story's reality. The chainsaw makes guests jump, but it destroys the scene's reality and breaks your spell. The post-chainsaw scenes suffer because the guests are about the "crazy rabbit guy." Keep your startles within the same world as your story.

THE CLIMAX

Build to a climax, don't leap to it. Imagine an emotional graph of any haunted attraction. The most successful ones look like a broken staircase. The intensity goes up, drops, and jumps higher at the next scare location, and drops again. When the intensity falls, it never returns to the same level as the resting moment before it. But, it's lower than the scare moment to allow guests to digest that scare and prepare for the next one.

This pattern continues until guests reach the highest level of fear (the climax). The climax is where "what everyone feared would happen" happens. Guests enter the "belly of the beast" and... discover hundreds of botched surgical remains or battle with the alien queen!

THE END...OR IS IT?

Now you've reached the scariest moment of the experience, and the haunt is over, right? WRONG. The middle is over, but you need a resolution. What's the impact or consequence of the series of horrible things that have happened? After the climax, guests must get back to the real world. If the climax is a trauma-inducing moment that then dumps guests into a gift shop, you undermine the story's reality.

Back to the homicidal surgeon... Climax: Guests discover the operating room filled with filleted corpses and misshapen, begging victims. Transition home: A quiet, hospital hallway lined in wanted posters for the surgeon. The posters suggest a villain still on the loose (material for next year), and the hallway transitions guests back to reality.

After the final connecting scene, you may add one final startle at the end. This is where most haunts use a chainsaw to chase the guests screaming out of the exit. Chainsaws are often force-fit into haunts because they're easy to do…but that's a different ebook.

Summary

Think of your haunt's story as a horror movie or first-person computer game. This structure is the "rising action" because, with each new element or scene, the stakes get a little higher. Rising action makes your guest's emotional journey more satisfying than random startles.

Every moment connects to your story. Contrast between key moments and connecting scenes to keep the rising action flowing. If the scare doesn't fit into the story, cut it. Go all out on the climax, but don't neglect the ending.

Finding Clues That Ignite Your Imagination

Now you understand the basic structure of a story, so let's take some time to explore how to fill that structure. Inspiration comes from about anywhere. The first thing to look at is your location. Let the building or field or tent inspire you. Walk through it at night with only a flashlight. When developing "The Vault of Souls," I let the vintage bank building lead the way. The restored bank lobby looked very elegant. The 11,000-square-foot basement was raw, filled with curving hallways, and had a real bank vault from the 1920s. It was almost as though the beginning and the middle of the story wrote themselves.

The Vault of Souls began at a high-end cocktail party celebrating the annual ritual that allowed guests to store their souls in the bank vault. The middle began as guests descended into the basement to explore and discover the paranormal residents from a time gone by. The ending was a real working speakeasy on the main floor. This gave a nice finale to the evening while still keeping within the era and elegance of the event.

Another great source of inspiration is local myths, folklore, or infamous history. I used quotes from the original bank president and photos of Tampa residents from the late 1920s to the 1940s in The Vault of Souls. These bits of reality anchored the story while acting as springboards for creating the backstory. If you use local history as inspiration, guests ask, "Did this actually happen?"

A bar I visited in New Orleans provided inspiration for the "After Hours" haunt at Busch Gardens. The reality of this bar inspired creepy scenes and propelled the story into a darker fictional mythology. The bar was a small, hidden place somewhere off Royal Street that claimed to be a vampire hangout. The decor was, as you might expect, contemporary Goth inspired. Everything was black or red. What intrigued me was this inconspicuous, unmarked little door at the end of one hallway. No one was monitoring the door, but, from time to time, regulars would walk down the hall and through the door. The most unusual thing was that I saw no one come out of that door. I began to wonder what blood-soaked debauchery was going on behind the door.

These fantasies inspired me to create a story about the fictional, after-hours "Club Muse," which catered to Goth wannabes. The twist—the lucky patrons who got into the VIP bar had their body parts harvested to create artwork. It was gross and creepy and never would have happened had I not been lucky enough to visit that vampire bar in the Big Easy.

Some of you may wonder if I ever mustered up enough courage to go through the door of that bar in New Orleans. The answer is no. I have no idea what was behind that door. It could have been an orgy of evil or an exit to the back alley. I don't care. The important thing is it inspired a cool haunted attraction!

In the next chapter, we'll explore how to use story to generate unique characters and scenes.

CHAPTER 2

Who Are Your Characters—Including Your Guests?

So, now you've learned the importance of story and have mapped out your journey. You know where you're starting, where you're going, and where you hope to end up. You understand the power of stories and how they affect the human experience. Now your goal is to fill that voyage with an ever-intensifying series of silence and screams—an ascending staircase of fear. Who will you meet along the way? Where will they hide? How will they reveal themselves? Remember, you're not afraid of the dark. You're afraid of what's in it.

Successful haunted attraction designers will tell you that actors make or break an event. One haunter even said, "Give me a candle and a cast of great performers, and we'll scare the crap out of you!"

In this chapter, we'll discuss how you use the plot to develop mind-blowing characters—characters who build on each other to create a tremendous trek through terror…and back.

SHARING THE BACKSTORY USING QUEUE CHARACTERS

To tell a rich story, you must give information about the world your guests are about to enter. From a character standpoint, this can be done with queue actors. I've seen queue actors who engage the guests but do little to set them up for the story of the haunt. This is a lost opportunity. Queue actors have time to spend with guests and thus an excellent opportunity to develop a relationship with them. Why not use these talented folks to start the storytelling process?

Queue characters whose actions and appearance begin to tell the story give your guests the tools to immerse themselves in it. Simple characters are fine. For the "Circus of Superstition" haunt at Howl-O-Scream, the queue character was a clown with a megaphone. He did what every circus barker has done since the beginning of circus—tempted guests with tidbits of information about the terrors that lay ahead. The story involved a touring circus of 13 superstitions presented by clowns; this direct approach worked well. The performer was energetic and worked the entire queue. He'd taunt guests to enter the Big Top by walking under a huge A-frame ladder—the first of the dreaded superstitions. (On a side note, it was amazing how many guests were reluctant or even refused to walk under the ladder. Superstitions are powerful, even in a make-believe context.)

We used a more subtle approach in the 2014 Howl-O-Scream haunt, "Deadfall." The story: the spirits of children inhabited a Victorian garden house where they used to play. The children were lonely and wanted to recruit more "playmates." The queue was a walkway through some tall rockwork. Perched high overhead was the ghost of a little girl in clothing from the 1800s. She was giggling and tossing white rose petals down onto the passing guests. Across the path from her was the ghost of a young boy in overalls perched high in the rockwork. Guests could hear him whistling a random tune as he sharpened a stick with his pocketknife. A contemporary gravedigger with a child-sized coffin sat next to the building's entrance. The gravedigger, oblivious to the spirits, warned guests, "Things ain't right in there."

We never used words to convey the backstory, but the actions of the queue characters set up the world for our guests to enter.

WHO ARE YOUR GUESTS?

Who are the guests walking through the haunt and how do they relate to the story? Address this character issue early. Are they inmates going through processing at a savage prison? Are they crew members abandoning ship after creatures took control of their star cruiser? Are they potential food for a ravenous family of hillbilly cannibals? Whatever you choose, avoid the option of "passive observers."

Giving your guests a role helps in two major ways:

1) It makes the experience more interactive for them.

2) Your performers have ways to engage the guests beyond the lame standbys: "Get Out!" "Arrgh!" and (the most offensive) "Boo!"

At The Vault of Souls, our guests are all treated as potential residents. The Exchange National Bank (the location of the event) developed a way to hold the souls of the departed in a vault for safe keeping. Bootleggers and gangsters filled Tampa in the 1920s, which made this service appealing.

From the moment they arrive, we treat our guests as you would any dignitary. After a cleansing of their aura, they're admitted to a posh cocktail reception in their honor. As the night progresses, they find more and more ways to unearth the stories of those who've come before them. By creating this environment for the guests, they behave in a certain way. They may not even realize it, but most of them play the part. Many even come in costumes from the 1920s. This increases the number of "characters" in the experience, making it richer.

Consider inexpensive giveaways to help clarify to your guests who they are. If you're doing an asylum theme, for example, you can give everyone a "patient wristband." The wristband defines the guest's character and is a "brag tag" they can use to promote your event after departing. Another example comes from a haunt I mentioned in the previous chapter, After Hours. This was a sinister nightclub, and I wanted guests to feel like patrons. Everyone received a hand stamp as they entered. The stamp was the mantra for the club, "MUSIC + PAIN = ART."

Another advantage to treating guests like characters is that you can sneak actors into your guest flow. These undercover performers widen your options. You can do things to these "guests" that you could never do to actual customers.

Here's a "victim concept" example that capitalizes on undercover performers. Actors dressed like patrons cycle through the queue (either at the beginning or at key locations). At the right moment, a character appears and snatches the "victim" from the queue (with much screaming in the darkness). If the victim has developed a relationship with the real guests in queue, this is even better.

I've often cast a young lady for this role. When she enters the queue, she tells the guests around her she's become separated from her friends. She claims to be scared and asks if she can go through the rest of the house with the guests she's chatting up. This simple interaction makes the capture so much more impactful.

I worried that the actor snatching the victim would grab an actual customer—which would be terrible! So, I had the victim actor wear a tee-shirt with a bulls-eye on the back and "VICTIM" in bold letters printed on the front. I was sure the real guests would notice, and the gimmick would be too obvious, but not one guest caught on. Some of the guests even asked the "victim" performers where they got their cool shirt.

CREATING THE BUILD THROUGH CHARACTERS

You've populated the beginning of your story with the right characters and given the customers an idea of their role. Now it's time to fill in the middle—the real heart of the story. Remember the middle is a series of ever-heightening moments leading to the climax. Many haunters plan this rising action based on the rooms. For example, guests first enter the kitchen and then proceed into a long hallway. Then they wander into the disgusting bathroom, etc. Others design their haunts based on the progression of characters that the guests encounter. First, the guests meet the carnies installing the Big Top, and then they must deal with the deformed stars of the Freak Show. After that, they're accosted by the whip-wielding animal trainer, etc. Both approaches work fine. In fact, character and scenic location are so closely connected that it's almost a chicken-or-egg scenario. The important thing to remember is that the story is the glue that holds these—and so many other—elements together. Story keeps everything moving forward and making sense.

So, let's talk about characters. Don't worry. We'll explore scenic development in much greater detail in the next chapter. The story has created the world, so the question you now need to ask is, "Who lives in this world?" The answer may seem obvious. If the story is about a prison, the characters are guards and prisoners. Unfortunately, a big haunt with only these two types of characters becomes repetitive. You need to dig deeper. Differentiate the prisoners based on their crimes: the first prisoners that guests encounter have committed lesser crimes. The seriousness of the crime builds throughout the haunt until the guests reach the isolation unit, home of the most dangerous serial killer. Meeting the most violent murderer would then become the climax of the story.

Another option might be to focus on the prison staff and make them the villains. You could create everything from sadistic guards to the prison psychologist who's busy hypnotizing inmates and turning them into mindless drones to the prison cafeteria workers who are filling the inmates' food with broken glass and live maggots. When guests meet the wicked warden, they discover that items crafted from the prisoners' severed body parts decorate his office. The warden's office would be the climax of this twisted tale.

Yet another approach to creating a build through character is to include a recurring persona who appears throughout the attraction. His or her identity becomes clearer each time guests see or hear them. In the prison scenario, consider an escaped inmate who's wreaking havoc throughout the facility. By using masks, matching costumes, and a recorded signature vocal (a laugh or a tune he hums), you can cast several actors to play the same character. This also creates the illusion that guests are being followed or chased throughout the haunt. The climax comes when the full character is revealed, and guests understand his sinister motives.

You can also use simple math to create rising action within your haunt. If one zombie is scary, ten zombies are terrifying! In our prison example: the confined population has become infested with a zombie plague. In the queue—which is in the prison exercise yard—guests encounter a lone zombie locked behind a chain-link fence. He's threatening, and helps set the scene, but he's not terrifying. In each room or cell block, guests encounter more and more zombies. As guests reach the execution room, they're surrounded by as many zombies as your budget allows. Zombies come from every direction, and guests see their shadows crawling across the overhead skylight (accomplished with a simple projection). This is the climax of this situation.

No matter your story, you must have a climax. The climax reveals what your guests fear most—the legions of zombies, the full embodiment of the character that's been following them, the blood-soaked carnage of the warden's office. The climax is the reason your guests took this journey. Anything you can do to enhance that moment will work to your advantage. This is the place to put some of your A-list actors. (Yes, the queue is the other one.) You should spare no expense on this scene. Make it unforgettable! This should be the moment that guests talk about on their drive home.

COMING BACK TO REALITY

You've told the story and revealed the climax, so now you ease your guests back into reality. Master haunter Joe Jensen once said, "All haunts have the same story— the journey to Hell and back." Many haunters are great about the "getting to Hell" part but often ignore the journey back. I get it. You fill the Hell of your haunt with the cool stuff, but, please, don't forget the transition back.

Try to use "callbacks" to the characters that guests have met along the way. For example, line the prison exit with framed photos of the warden shaking hands with city officials and accepting rehabilitation awards. Or, guide guests through the prison emergency exit as they hear a recognizable laugh from the shadows. This gives your guests a chance to reflect on their experience. It also lulls them into a sense of security and tells them the show is over. Standard procedure suggests that you'd then have one final startle performer to send them out the door screaming…and I'm OK with that.

In the next chapter, we'll examine how to design scenery, lighting, audio, costumes, and makeup that reinforce the story. I'll share some examples from my experience and toss out some new ideas.

CHAPTER 3

Crafting the Story by Creating the Atmosphere

Startled awake, you believe you've heard a muffled scream. As your mind comes into focus, you remember that you're a guest in a Victorian manor. Looking around the antiquated room, you hear the sound of breaking glass coming from next door. You creep out of bed and head into the hallway. After a couple of knocks on the neighbor's door, you call out, "Is everything all right in there?" There's no response.

Knocking harder, you shout, "Is everything all right?" Your hand reaches for the doorknob, and you discover it's unlocked. As the door creaks open, you feel a chill. At first you believe it's your paranoia, but then you notice the shattered, full-length window. The cold night air is blowing the wispy curtains inward. An odd aroma that's both sweet and foul fills the moonlit room—the combined scent of roses and decay.

Adjusting to the pale light, you notice the outline of a female figure curled up on the floor. Without understanding why, you kneel next to her and touch her exposed arm. She's colder than death. She's wearing a white satin nightgown, and her dressing gown is laid neatly across the foot of the bed. As you roll her onto her back, her head falls to one side, revealing two fresh puncture wounds in her neck. Your head floods with images of blood and dark folklore. The lifeless body twitches. You look down with a spark of hope. Her eyes snap open to reveal two glowing red embers, and she smiles slowly to reveal a mouthful of jagged teeth. She lunges toward your face with a growling hiss. All goes silent and black.

Readers experience these stories with their senses. The detailed descriptions conjure an experience in the reader's mind. The same is true with haunted attractions or any kind of atmospheric performance. The more the scenic elements reinforce the plot, the more guests feel they're part of the story. Guests react more to characters who look like inhabitants of their world. The lighting, audio, and (yes) scent design act as the track to the guests' emotional roller-coaster ride. These are the elements we'll focus on in this chapter.

WHERE ARE WE?

Let's start with scenery—which is costly—so every dime and minute spent on it must contribute to the plotline. One of the first decisions you need to make as a designer is the layout of the haunt's pathway and the progression of rooms. When doing this, keep in mind the basic story structure that we discussed in the first two chapters.

Each story has:

- A beginning, in which you share exposition and backstory.
- A middle filled with a series of events that become more intense.
- A climax, which is the most impactful and memorable moment or the reason the story is being told.
- An ending, which contains the falling action and the return to reality.

Even the pathway and the size and shape of the rooms themselves can contribute to the story you're trying to tell.

In 2010, I wrote and directed a haunt at Busch Gardens' Howl-O-Scream in Tampa called *"Alone."* To my knowledge, this was the first time a theme park had installed a haunt that guests could experience by themselves. The layout and entrance were critical to maintain the intimacy. Guests met a blind security guard, passed through the chain-link gate of Minotaur Storage, and then walked down a winding, tree-lined pathway. At last, they came to the structure's entrance. This area was quiet and had no performers. I wanted the patron to feel like they were leaving the security of the raucous, theme-park event and entering the world of collector Alexander Daedalus.

This haunt had a safe word that guests could use to end the experience and return to the real world. You'd be surprised (I know I was) how many people used the safe word while walking down that empty dark pathway. Walking into the unknown established the atmosphere of the abandoned warehouse better than dialogue or animation.

At the end of the walk, guests met a large, lobotomized man-child who pointed to a group of chairs. Everyone took a seat. He played a recording on an old cassette player that explained the backstory and instructions to the guests. Having the guests take seats was another way of establishing control. Being seated reduces your sense of control and makes you feel more subservient. This feeling was an important part of the story and an effective way of conveying it.

Other pathway considerations include the size of each room. Do you want a space to seem imposing or claustrophobic? Safety will dictate some of this, but there are ways to create these illusions of space or lack of it. If you're indoors, and you want a space to seem grand or open, make sure the ceiling is matte black. This way, when guests look up, it will seem to them they're looking into an infinite depth.

TRICKS FOR CREATING A SENSE OF SPACIOUSNESS...OR CLAUSTROPHOBIA

Open spaces are often used for grand facades. I once did a haunted ballroom that I wanted to appear huge, but it had low ceilings. The solution was to expand the room horizontally by adding mirrors to all the walls. Half columns hid the mirrors' seams, so they appeared full when the reflection created the other half. Hooded mannequins (and actors wearing the same costume) corralled guests throughout the space. Guests felt outnumbered.

What about ADA width and height regulations, you ask? I have a couple of suggestions. To make the hallway appear narrower, hang large tapestries parallel to the walls. It makes the hallway feel tighter around guests' heads while still leaving the appropriate width around their feet. The most common solution to this situation is to use inflatable walls. I've always loved this effect, but make sure there's a justification in your story for such a bold installation.

One idea I used was to have guests enter a closet filled with heavy coats. The further they pushed into the closet, the darker it got. When the lighting was at its lowest, the inflatable walls began. After pushing their way through, guests emerged into a parallel universe. We called it the "Narnia" closet.

To close in the ceiling of a hallway, install two-by-fours every two to three feet, placing them perpendicular to the walls at exactly 6'4" from the ground. (This is the ADA rule for height.) The sprinkler system still operates but, from the guests' perspective, it creates a low ceiling. If it's dark above the pergola you've created, that's even better! I'm sure there are many more ways to use your pathway design to tell your story.

CREATING MOOD WITH DISTRESSING
AND DETAILS

When you start to install walls and props, make sure they're finished in such a way that they enhance the story. We all know about aging and distressing scenery, but you must "distress with a purpose." Are your walls weathered or immaculate? Your story determines it. What happened to cause that huge blood stain on the floor or that filthy spot on the wall? Thoughtlessly splattering faux blood or dry-brushing dirty marks does nothing for your story. In fact, it makes the area look fake and takes the guests out of the world you're trying to create.

In an asylum haunt I wrote, we scratched horizontal gashes along the narrow hallway walls. The gashes communicated details of the story (someone being dragged against their will). The art director used a four-pronged garden tool to make the gashes (we don't claw with our thumbs). We glued torn fingernails into the gashes and added some paint work to finish the wallpaper.

Another way we distressed with a purpose was in a prison setting. There was a drinking fountain installed as a scenic piece in the visitation room. This was an early room in the haunt, and I wanted to reinforce the penitentiary's cruelty. I asked the scenic team to make it look as though someone had vomited in the drinking fountain—a visiting guest, upon hearing horrific news about one of the prisoners, had vomited. The vomit's dryness reinforced the terrible conditions of this facility. In fact, it turned out so well that we added a practical light over the top so more guests could see it. Subtle details aren't noticed by everyone, but they ensnare those who do into your story.

SETTING THE STYLE WITH COSTUMES AND MAKEUP

Story also determines your character's clothing and makeup. First, decide the period of your story. Does it take place in present day? Is the story set in Victorian England? Is it set in the 1970s? (Yes, I've seen some 3D disco haunts.) The period determines the style of the clothing and the conditions.

Many haunts set their plotline in the present day because it makes finding costumes and props easier. Because The Vault of Souls is set in 1923, many of the characters are ghosts from that era. So, our costumes must be period-specific and not distressed—ghosts don't age. If your story is set in present day, but your characters are immortal vampires from the 1800s, distress the clothing. Clothing wears out after 200 years of use. Correct costuming transports both characters and guests to the appropriate place and time.

Once you have a costume's era, make it look like your character has worn it since then. Often, you'll need to distress costumes just as you do the scenery. Again, distress with purpose. Since a story is a progression of actions and events, it's best to have the costumes progress as well. If the story is about a zombie invasion, the costumes decay as the guests move through the haunt. This not only provides variety, but it also reinforces the build of your story. Have the costumes disintegrate to show the zombies are becoming savage, or soak them in blood to indicate the zombies are devouring human flesh.

When distressing costumes, it's necessary to ask a few basic questions: Whose blood is it? Is the character bleeding, or is the blood from their victims? The placement and splatter pattern communicate that to your guests. What tore the clothing or why did it wear out in a certain place? "Running through barbed wire" tears are different from "brutal werewolf attack" tears.

I'm sure some of you reading this are thinking, "No one will ever notice these things! Why waste the time?" I used to believe that, too, and then I read a study that showed humans are far more aware of details than we realize. We process more information than we're aware of. Oftentimes, "gut feelings" occur after our subconscious processes certain information. In other words, the details affect our guests whether they realize it or not.

CREATING MOOD WITH LIGHT AND SOUND

Work with your lighting designers to answer the same kinds of story-driven questions: "Where's the light coming from? Is the dim forest path lit by moonlight or lamplight from the cabin's window?" The angle and color of your lighting change depending on what makes sense for the story.

Audio works the same way. Use audio "beds" of low, ambient, sound effects to create an environment. In one house I wrote many years ago, I had the sound of doves cooing at key locations throughout the house. Not only is this a creepy sound, it also reinforced the story (which was about a murderous motorcycle gang that left a dead dove on top of each of its victims). In another example, I used a bed of "muffled passing trains" to help set the tone of a subway haunt.

Lighting and audio are often overlooked when designing a haunt. Don't get caught in the "make it loud, make it dark" trap. Use these great storytelling tools to their fullest effect.

With your story written, your cast ready, and your house built, what next? You use story to shape your marketing plans! Social media strategy, merchandise sales, and even up-sell opportunities must all tie to story.

CHAPTER 4

The Dénouement— Turning Your Story Into a Memory

Stories need a blast-off, twists and turns to pique interest, an appealing climax, and then falling action. Falling action, or dénouement, returns the audience to the world of reality. This chapter is that falling action. So far, we've explored developing a story and using that story to materialize your haunt. Now, we'll discuss how story inspires the Three M's—marketing, merchandise, and munchies.

When story influences the Three M's of an attraction, the result enthralls guests. This is a concept that major theme parks learned a long time ago and continue to apply. It guarantees that guests arrive informed and leave with a souvenir. Are guests watching your characters for only one day or evening, or are they learning about your characters before they arrive, eating their food, and leaving with a piece of their world? Both Disney and Universal Studios are masters at this kind of immersion. Two examples of immersion are "Radiator Springs" at Disney's California Adventure and Universal Studio's "Wizarding World of Harry Potter." I had nothing to do with either, but I draw a great deal of inspiration from their seamless storytelling. (If you can visit them, I urge it!)

Most haunts can't commit the time or money that the big theme parks do to the Three M's. But, with savvy planning, we can all apply some of their successful ideas.

MARKETING THE PROLOGUE

OK, let's break down how you can use story to drive revenue. First, use your pre-event marketing to start your story before your guests arrive. You can "leak" information about the Halloween season long before the leaves fall. Use social media to drop compelling hints or tidbits of the backstory.

Here's an example. The first post on Facebook for The Vault of Souls was on February 13th, 2015 (yes, it was a Friday). This was eight months before the event opened its doors for the first time. We began discreetly. The very first post was, "Shhhh..." The first profile picture was a single finger held up to a pair of lips. More than four years later, that Facebook page is almost another character in the story. The page's "voice" represents the spirits that live within The Exchange National Bank. Posts are almost always cryptic and rarely use punctuation or capital letters. This helps set the tone for the paranormal event and aligns with the story. This past year, "the spirits" dropped clues in the form of ciphers, which the followers rapidly decoded. Using interactive storytelling, the page has 3,000 followers engaging throughout the year.

Once the primary marketing campaign kicks in, continue to use your story as the inspiration for your content. Guests enjoy seeing an event's theme played out in its advertising. Since you're creating mythology (versus relying on intellectual properties), you can use marketing to teach guests about it. If you have a central character, define him/her and include them in your print and video media. The more depth the character has, the more people will become fascinated. I like to think of the marketing strategy as the first impression of any haunt. As we've all heard for years, "You never get a second chance to make the right first impression."

Because haunts have limited budgets, you must be wise with advertising spend. There are many schools of thought on how to divide the money between product and marketing. Some think you should spend the lion's share on advertising to "get the butts in the seats." Others rely on word of mouth and invest more in the product. I'm not sure it's wise to separate these two elements. In my mind, the marketing and the product are twins. They stem from the same story. If your haunt harmonizes with the promotional elements, your guests feel more encouraged to visit. My experience shows they're also more likely to recommend the event to their friends. This means you get the most out of your advertising efforts.

One useful tool is to create a "spokescharacter." This character is useful for oodles of outreach: in-studio visits to the local news media, off-property appearances at targeted gatherings, and even "unexpected' appearances in public. (A word of caution: Use your best judgment and check your local laws before trying this one. Startle responsibly.) This character should evolve from your story but may not be your main villain. I know this sounds counter-intuitive,but hear me out. If your main character is a crazed, flesh-eating clown, the nature of his character dictates that he won't be able to share any of the crucial facts and figures about your event (dates, times, where to get tickets, etc.). Also, when you take the killer clown out of his environment, he loses his mystique. He becomes "a guy in a costume." You want to build a sense of suspense, not diminish it. If you take this character into the real world, he should be able to live in it. That way, he can bridge the gap between reality and the nightmare you've created.

Many years ago, at Busch Gardens' Howl-O-Scream, we had a main character who was a killer cab driver. We knew that if we sent him out on media appearances, he'd be laughable. So, instead of sending the cab driver himself, we sent some of his victims. These were characters who'd fled his taxi with their lives. They'd seen the face of evil and could relay it to potential guests. For The Vault of Souls, we sent out performers dressed in 1920s attire wearing neutral, white-face masks and carrying large, black, glowing umbrellas. Traveling with these slow-moving, silent characters was a somber person dressed in black formalwear. He answered questions and guided these wayward spirits back to the other side by ringing a bell. These characters drew attention, thereby advertising the event and reinforcing the story.

Another interesting and effective marketing tool is the "media gift." This is a small token that you deliver to local media personalities. If it's cool and ties to your story, DJs and reporters may talk about it for weeks. Even better, they may display it on their set throughout the Halloween season. This happened one year when we were promoting a vampire-themed concept. I created pictures of local news personalities as vampires and then delivered the photos in themed frames. (Always include a logo; otherwise, viewers may confuse your event with a competitor.) One daily talk show displayed the photos of its team on the bookshelves behind the anchor desk. Every time the camera was on the reporter, our logo was over her shoulder. We couldn't have asked for anything better!

With creative brainstorming, you can come up with a plethora of story-based marketing ideas. Make sure the ideas communicate the basic information about your business and reinforce the plot of your story. You must meet both criteria for the ideas to be effective. If you work this into the creative development of your event, it will all flow together.

EATING AND DRINKING WITHIN YOUR CREATED WORLD

Don't overlook the food. Anything that ties food and beverage offerings into your story improves the guest experience. It also encourages sales.

Most haunts I've visited that serve alcohol have a themed "signature" drink. These drinks range from pre-packaged, test-tube shots to a hand-crafted, blood-red cocktail called "The Sacred Contract." Don't overlook locally brewed beer and wine products with haunt-themed names (i.e., "Dead Guy Ale" and "Vampire" wine. I have no affiliation with either of these brands; I'm mentioning them here as examples.) Whether or not you choose to sell alcohol, offer a drink that's themed to your event. Several companies provide customizable plastic cups and sippers in all shapes and sizes. I've seen these sell very well. Don't leave this potential money on the table.

As far as food goes, there are several easy ways to tie this to your concept. For example, if you have a "Day of the Dead" theme, why not work out a deal with a local taco truck. Set them up in your parking lot, help them decorate, and split the revenue. If your story involves a cannibalistic hillbilly family, offer a helping of "Granny Grotesque's Down Home Chili." I'd imagine this would be popular in colder climates. If your story revolves around a parcel of creepy children, offer vintage candy for sale in the queue. These food suggestions reinforce the story, quench guests' hunger, and make money.

SOMETHING TO REMEMBER THE JOURNEY

The current consumer trend is that buyers want to spend money on experiences rather than on objects. So, you may ask, why am I suggesting selling merchandise at your haunt? Because, if the merchandise you sell ties to your story, guests will buy things to remind them of their experience.

Years ago, we used to say that every haunt should have a basic "$10 tee-shirt" (nowadays, a "$20 tee-shirt"). This was a simple shirt with the event logo and year. These shirts were a cheap souvenir—and a great marketing tool. Guests are becoming more and more savvy about this concept, so they may or may not buy this shirt. I still pick one up because I like the brag tag-quality of wearing shirts from haunts I've visited. Or, offer a shirt that looks like it might be a costume from the event or even something a character wore. If you have an asylum theme, for example, you could offer a staff shirt or an inmate shirt from that asylum. If you offer both, couples might buy them as Halloween costumes! If you sell tee-shirts, have at least one design that's a female cut. Many women won't buy a tee-shirt that's the standard, unisex style. Also, if you can afford to keep the stock, offer XXL and XXXL sizes. If you need to charge more for the extended sizes, do it; most folks are OK paying a little more for them. Many screen-printing companies can supply whatever style shirt you want to sell at reasonable prices. Google these vendors or check out any of the haunt trade shows.

Themed photos are also a viable merchandise option. The thing is, these snaps need to be fresh and unique to your story. Anyone can take a selfie, but only you can provide an exclusive frame overlay. If you have a ghost-town theme, the overlay could be a vintage "wanted" poster. If your story takes place in a morgue, the overlay could be a death certificate. You're only limited by your imagination. Take photos in the queue for viewing on the exit monitor. If printing is too expensive, sell digital copies delivered via email (which also builds your email database).

Does this seem like too much work? Investigate outside companies that can do this for you. Some even work on revenue splits. Never miss the chance to sell guests something they might use to promote your haunt.

Other merchandise options to personalize for your story include: lanyards, phone cases, shot glasses, hats, etc. Online companies like Vistaprint or Zazzle offer huge product lines.

A well-crafted story produces gobs of ideas to help your guests continue their journey.

NOW IT'S YOUR TURN TO CONTINUE THE STORYTELLING TRADITION

From the cavemen family huddled around the campfire to the latest in augmented reality, storytelling is part of what makes us human. We're wired to receive and remember information. Stories fill our lives with memories, both real and imagined. I hope this little book has given you a better understanding of how to use storytelling in the entertainment industry—and, especially, in haunted attractions.

I look forward to seeing what the future holds, but I know it will involve a story.

About the Publisher

Philip Hernandez is a freelance writer, speaker, producer, and marketer specializing in Seasonal Attractions.

In 2018, Philip became the CEO at Gantom Lighting & Controls, a manufacturer of the world's smallest DMX LED lighting. Gantom is used in every major theme park worldwide to illuminate where other fixtures cannot. Watch Gantom Illuminate: www.gantom.com

Since 2014 Philip has published Seasonal Entertainment Source magazine (SES), a quarterly print publication for the seasonal attraction professional. SES ships to readers in over 18 countries. Read articles here: www.seasonalentertainmentsource.com

Philip operates the Haunted Attraction Network (HAN), the largest global media entity for the haunted attraction industry. HAN includes written content, videos, a series of podcasts, and the Haunt Design Kit brand.

Visit HAN here:

www.hauntedattractionnetwork.com

Philip produces the Leadership Symposium for Seasonal Attractions, a masterclass series for seasonal attraction professionals.

Watch more here:

https://youtu.be/U4Vz8jNw_EQ

Philip co-hosts the 'Marketing your Attraction' podcast monthly.

Listen here:

www.marketingyourattraction.com

Contact Philip for projects here:

hernandez.philip@gmail.com

About the Cover Artist

DOUG SCHAEFER

Horror and FX artist, Production Manager for Robot Monkey Lab, Inc. and creator of two books of art. Doug has been creating effects, props, masks and artwork for haunted attractions, theme parks and collectors for over 30 years. By day Doug designs and builds effects, puppets and illusions at Robot Monkey Lab, Inc (VFXcreates.com). And on evenings and weekends Doug makes even more monsters, in his home studio (ArtGuyDesigns.com), creating a variety of horror and creature art.

About the Author

For over 30 years, **Scott Swenson** has been bringing stories to life as a Writer, Director, Producer and Performer. His work in Theme Park, Consumer Events, Live Theater and Television has given him a broad spectrum of experiences. After 21 years working with SeaWorld Parks and Entertainment as the Director of Production, Scott formed *Scott Swenson Creative Development LLC.* Since then he has been writing live shows, creating and implementing themed festivals and developing communication based training classes. Much of Scott's work has focussed on seasonal entertainment. He was co-creator and Creative Leader for the first 15 years of the "Howl-O-Scream" event at Busch Gardens Tampa, during which time he wrote and implemented over 50 haunted houses, shows and scare zones. From 2014 to 2017, he was the Writer and Creative Director for the historically based atmospheric theatre piece, "The Vault of Souls".

Scott has also written and consulted for haunted attractions at Valleyfair Theme Park, SeaWorld Texas and ZooTampa. His most recent projects include "DARK" at Fort Edmonton Park in Edmonton, Alberta Canada and "UNDead in the Water" at The American Victory Ship in Tampa. He is a regular contributor to "Seasonal Entertainment Source" magazine and his podcast, "A Scott in the Dark" continues to grow in popularity. In his "free time" Scott has self published 3 books of dark poetry and prose. In 2017 he was presented a Special Recognition Award from The Haunted Attraction Association for his "…unprecedented investment and support for the haunted attraction industry." He is a sought after panelist and presenter for Entertainment trade shows, especially those focused on haunted attractions and atmospheric theatre.